A Vietnamese Pilgrimage

Max Ediger

Faith and Life Press
Newton, Kansas

ii

Library of Congress Number 78-53650
International Standard Book Number 0-87303-007-9
Printed in the United States of America
Copyright © 1978 by Faith and Life Press
718B Main Street, Newton, Kansas 67114

Design by John Hiebert
Printing by Mennonite Press, Inc.

Introduction

The war is over now in Viet Nam, but the struggle continues. As people work in their fields, some are still maimed and others killed by munitions lying unexploded in their fields. To shape and create a new society—to reconstruct a new nation—requires an intense struggle. The cost is high. Refugees are still being created by the force of events. While some flee, others yearn to return but cannot. Fighting continues in the area, now between Viet Nam and Cambodia. There is much economic suffering. Food is very scarce. And some of the freedoms which were part of the earlier Viet Nam are not a part of the Viet Nam today.

"When and how will we live as one happy family?" asks Max Ediger in this poetic recreation of his Vietnamese experience. The outlook is rather bleak. The U.S. Congress refuses to give even food aid to hungry people in Viet Nam. Some Americans give through Mennonite Central Committee and Church World Service, but most are silent.

What kind of concern can Christians in Canada and the United States show besides praying for suffering people in Viet Nam and for the church there? We can urge our respective governments to give reconstruction assistance either directly to Viet Nam or through United Nations agencies. We can give food and funds to help Viet Nam rebuild through private agencies such as MCC and CWS.

The American people have tried to forget Viet Nam without coming to terms with what happened there. The drama of what happened pulsates in the pages of this book. Read and reflect. Allow the feeling of Max's *Vietnamese Pilgrimage* to throb in your being.

Vern Preheim
Mennonite Central Committee
Akron, Pennsylvania

iii

Preface

"But now abide faith, hope, love these three; but the greatest of these is love."
1 Corinthians 13:13, NASB.

There are many events in history which are extremely complex and require lengthy and deep research to ferret out the truth: if indeed it is possible to actually find the truth. The Viet Nam war is one of those situations. It is up to the historians who have the time and discipline to wade through volumes of documents, to come up with the final analysis of what really happened in the Viet Nam conflict. I am not one of those historians. This book is rather a pilgrimage through five years of living and learning in Viet Nam.

It is difficult for us to look at ourselves and our responsibilities in complex situations. If we can focus attention on the possible or actual abrogation of human rights by others, we can avoid dealing with our own violations of human rights. It is easier to point at others than to look inside ourselves. My pilgrimage in Viet Nam was an experience of looking at myself and my Christian community. I began to realize that only when I am open to seeing my own life's inconsistencies and dealing with them, can I honestly speak out about the inconsistencies of those outside myself and my community. It was a pilgrimage of self-discovery and self-revelation.

Previous to my pilgrimage in Viet Nam, I had never written poetry, and my experience in writing prose was limited to one course in college. I remember very clearly the situation which drove me to pen my first poem. I had not been in Viet Nam long, and it was all still very strange and new to me. For the first time in my life I was seeing real violence. I witnessed the brutality of war as I saw villages destroyed by air strikes, schools shattered by rockets, and bodies lying lifeless among the ruins. The welling up of emotions within me was like a geyser which must find release somehow. My release came through writing down my feelings in verse form. I was surprised at what I had done, but I also knew that it made me feel better. And so, from then on, I wrote whenever I needed release. Sometimes I needed to express my fear and sorrow; sometimes it was anger, and other times it was joy.

My pilgrimage through Viet Nam brought me in touch with many people who helped me and shared with me. The Mennonite Central Committee community in Viet Nam helped me keep in touch with priorities and values. They were always a source of Christian love and encouragement. Three Vietnamese co-workers also were a special part of that pilgrimage. Hang, full of life and creativity, gave me much encouragement, guidance and enthusiasm in my struggle to express my feelings. Tin, a young Mennonite, seemed to have a strength and assurance which always gave inspiration. Tieu was the quiet, inconspicuous person who showed a gentle compassion which brought real human kindness into this often hectic and violent life.

Another close friend, Manh Tuong, had the special gift of asking questions, and could always offer encouragement when I was feeling overcome by the situation. He encouraged me to write, and always told me that a valuable experience should not be kept selfishly to oneself, but should be shared so that others could also benefit from it. Manh Tuong introduced me to Buu Chi a young artist. For several years I knew Buu Chi only through his art work as he was locked away in a dark prison cell. Without words, his art—which was secretly slipped out of prison—eloquently spoke to me of his life and his dreams. With the war's end, he was freed from prison and our meeting was like the reunion of two old friends. What joy to see him a free person! Some of his art work is shared in this book.

vi

These and many other friends were my teachers and companions through this pilgrimage. I hope that as you read this book, you will feel a more personal acquaintance with these people. It is very important that we do not let political, economic, or religious differences interfere with the formation of sharing relationships. Christians have been called to serve "in the name of Christ," and that means opening ourselves to others and being willing to take the risk of going on pilgrimages. It is my hope that as we go on our various pilgrimages, we will be drawn together in a closer community of Christian love, and peace will become a reality.

Contents

vii

1975

viii

1976

1971

6. 8. 1974. Bunchi

The dusty plains of Oklahoma did not prepare me well for the savagery of war which I was to experience in Viet Nam. Shortly after my arrival I experienced the realities of bombs and rockets. As I stood among the rubble of schools and homes and helped pick up the mutilated bodies of the victims of this unwanted war, my mind churned with emotions and thoughts I had never experienced before. The only release from this agony was to write down my feelings so that I would never forget them.

The War Is Winding Down

I
The war is winding down
  (so they say).
It's not an issue anymore.
We're moving our men out
  (and our bombs in).
American lives aren't being lost
  much anymore.
"Let Asians kill Asians,"
that's our cry.
It hurts less to read about
  Asian death statistics.
"It's their war, let them fight it!"
  (Is it?)
At least we've done our part to help.
Perhaps there are a few bad side effects:
  broken families,
  destroyed homes and lands,
  lost customs and traditions,
  prostitution,
  mutilated men, women, and children,
  fear, hate, anger, distrust,
  people dehumanized by refugee camps,
  torture.
Still, we deserve some thanks for
  our help.
Never mind though;
we have work to do.

3

We must get ready for the
    next war.
There will be one you know.
We haven't repented yet.

II
He said,
"You speak of love,
And I see
    my home bombed,
    my family napalmed,
    my country destroyed.
    Hate!"
I said (meekly),
"But we still
    love you."
He said,
"If this is the result
    of your love,
then take it elsewhere.
It's creating a
    hell for us."

III
"Give unto Caesar
that which is Caesar's"
we often quote.
When Caesar requests,
we pay up.
But few seem very interested in what
    really belongs to Caesar.
You see, Caesar has ways of
    encouraging us.
"If I don't pay my phone tax, I may
    lose my phone."
"If I don't pay the war tax, I may
    lose my home
        or
    go to prison
(and that's no place for a Christian)."

"If I protest, I'm not
  patriotic."
So we pay up, and other people lose
  their homes,
  their possessions,
  their lives.
It's easier that way.
(Perhaps it's the Christian responsibility.)
". . . And unto God
that which is God's."
How safe it is to skip over
  that phrase.
If we don't, there is
  conflict.
Maybe Caesar is asking for
  what really is God's.
Who gets it?
We say,
"Everything I have belongs
  to God."
If that's true, what can Caesar
  demand from us?
Can he demand
  our money?
  our complete, unquestionable dedication?
  our lives?
  the right to choose our friends and enemies?
The question then is,
Whom do we really serve?
  Caesar?
  God?
We don't have to answer;
the world already knows.
The world can see.

IV
In the beginning
  God created.
In the end
  man destroyed.

V
There is one, and only one way
   to stamp out evil and wrong
   and bring peace.
FORCE AND VIOLENCE.
It has always worked in the past
and it will continue to work
   in the future.
And a still small voice says,
"What about My way?"

VI
We pray,
"God, protect our soldiers
   in Viet Nam."
"God, bring peace to the
   world."
Then we write out our checks to
   IRS,
knowing that the biggest part
   of those checks
will be used to
send soldiers out to be killed
   and to
continue the war.

VII
He planted it near the road.
The soil hid its small gray form;
the root of its life stretched across the path.
It waited, expectantly,
for all elements to be present,
so it could burst into life.

A man appeared.
The root of life was triggered.
The gray form burst into life.
It threw back the covering of soil
and reached out to achieve the end
for which it had been created.

Its bloom was death;
its fragrance rotting flesh and blood;
its life was very short,
but effective and complete.
It did the work without hesitation
which its creator had designed it for.

How much better to plant flowers.

VIII
Yesterday I saw his family altar.
It was small and simple.
On it were three pictures:
two pictures were of his mother and father;
the center picture, his brother.
Only he is left alive to keep the incense burning.
His brother died in battle;
his parents were killed by a bomb.
At fifteen he is alone in the world,
a world which appears to him evil and terrifying.
I feel I must speak to him.
I must tell him,
"I did not kill your family.
This is not my war, I cannot accept it.
I will not fight in it;
I will not pay for it;
I will forever speak against it."
But can he hear?
Now in his sorrow and despair
can I expect him to listen and understand?
I am too late!
The war has turned into a monster
which consumes all.
Had I spoken sooner,
had I faced God's challenge when I accepted His leadership,
this war could have been avoided.
Then he could have heard;
then he could have understood;
then he would still have his family.

God can forgive me,
but can my brother?
I have failed;
this small family altar is bitter proof of that.
Let this be my confession
before God and the world.
Now I accept God's challenge;
now I am ready to deal with the world
on God's terms.
Perhaps it is not too late,
but it is late.

X

A shattered primary school:
blood and splintered desks littering the floor,
mutilated bodies of small children,
terror in the eyes of the survivors,
long funeral processions,
hysterical parents burying their small boys—
all because of one small rocket.
What must be the results of a bomb
dropped from thirty thousand feet
on a school building full
of eager young children?
Does guilt become greater
as the death toll increases?
If so, those who make, and drop
the seven-ton bombs
have a great guilt to repent of.
But perhaps, rather, the guilt becomes greater
with increase in knowledge.
Some of us know
about loving one's neighbor,
God is love.
Perhaps we are the ones
who have the greatest sin.

Nguyen, a nineteen-year-old student, became one of my closest friends during the early part of my pilgrimage. His struggle to comprehend why God would let this war grind on and on and pit brother and sister against each other touched me deeply. Nguyen was just about to finish the twelfth year of school and was preparing to take exams for entrance into the university when the South Vietnamese government changed the draft law so that any young man in high school who was nineteen years of age or older had to enter the army. He told me that he was going to join the navy so that he would not have to be involved in direct combat and fight against his own people. While trying to make these arrangements, he drowned in the ocean. Only a short time after his death, the law was once again changed, and he would have been allowed to finish his high school and go on to college. As I sat with his family at the funeral, I tried to understand why this young man, so brilliant, sensitive and caring, had to die so early in life and so senselessly.

A Student's Prayer

Chorus
Grant me wisdom,
grant me peace;
for I have heard
of Your love way.
I am weak
and I am blind
I need some help
to find the way.

1: I look around me;
I see destruction.
O Lord, You know how much
I want to believe.
But every time
a flower blooms,
someone finds a way
to destroy it.

2: People talk about
new ways of living,
how their religion
brings people together.
But when the threats come
they join in the battle.
Is religion only
for times of quiet?

3: They say that it's done
in love and in Your name—
that the war is meant
to free and preserve us.
I see my homeland
bloodred and crying.
Why must Your love
be so terrifying?

4: All their words now
fall on my deaf ears.
If they won't live it,
then I won't hear it.
For all their words
are only vibrations;
but actions show
the god they worship.

5: I tell my friends
I have no religion.
I've tried so many
yet found them lacking.
I know You're living
but I can't find You.
Why must I die
with my search unended?

Sometimes hopelessness overtook people as they tried vainly to see a bright place in their future. Thuan, a young student, expressed such fear and loneliness in this poem which he wrote for a close friend who had just been killed by the war.

Fire Consumes Our Village *

Fire consumes our village;
our proud homeland lies in ruins.
I see tears in the old mother's eyes;
days of hope are shattered.

In days past, with blue eyes and innocent minds
we cheerfully carried our sad fate.
In days past, with childlike laughter and tears,
we entered a sad and lonely plight.

Today, I hear you have fallen.
I am still here to mourn for you,
for a Viet Nam in total desolation—
for a humanity which is lost.

Thuan

10

* Translated from Vietnamese

1972

One day the local daily paper carried the story of a young man who was killed as he tried to steal a watch. The article ended with the statement that the owner got his watch back. As I walked through the discouraging, crowded refugee camps, I wondered how many of the young children there would someday find themselves forced into thievery and prostitution in order to survive. Would one of these bright-eyed little children be killed so that a watch could be returned to an owner?

So Shines the Sun

Sunlight streamed through the foliage above his head. Only dimly aware of the shafts of light playing games over his face, Sung's mind began to wander. Perhaps catalyzed by the light rays dancing over his eyes, his mind went back in time.

I.

The sun hung lazily in the sky above the small village. The heat bore down on the small collection of houses and the surrounding rice paddies, but despite the heat, everywhere people were at work harvesting the rice that would feed them during the coming months. At noon a drum began to beat, and the children poured out of the schoolrooms into the courtyard. The air was filled with their shouts and laughter as they headed down the various paths leading to their homes. It was time for dinner and a short rest from the heat.

Eight-year-old Sung ran laughing down the path that led to the group of thatched houses where he lived with his parents and little sister. He could see his father coming in from the rice field where he had been working all morning. Usually his mother also worked in the rice field, but she had recently given birth to Sung's little sister and was not yet strong enough to go to the fields. Entering the house, Sung bowed slightly with arms folded and greeted his grandmother. She was there to take care of his mother and to make the food. It was the responsibility of the family to provide a place for her to live and food to eat in her old age, and they did so gladly. In return she would help out in the house and often direct the household activities. Being the oldest member of the family she was given great respect because of her age and wisdom.

When Sung's father entered the house he went to the family altar, lit three sticks of incense and bowed three times. Sung watched closely because he knew the time would come when he would be expected to keep the altar and offer prayers to the ancestors. When his own parents died he must know how to show the proper respect so that their spirits would be happy.

Sung often dreamed of the day when he would work in the fields and take care of the graves of the ancestors. This land had belonged to his family for many generations and he was proud that he would be able to improve the farm and work it more efficiently. Sung was already being trained for the day when all this would be his responsibility.

"Some of the farmers say that we must be careful of the airplanes," Sung's father was saying as the family ate its meal of rice and vegetables. "There are many soldiers here now and the foreigners do not like them. Mr. Nhung says that the big planes have dropped bombs in Son Loc village and he thinks they may come here someday."

"But we have done nothing to them," Sung's mother replied angrily. "Can't they leave us alone in peace?"

Sung had heard this many times before. There was always talk about the war, but he could not really understand it. Often the great silver planes raced overhead, but they held a fascination for Sung. He did not understand where they were going or what they were doing. Someday he hoped they would come close enough so he could see them better.

"Please Father, Mother, Grandmother. I am going to school now. Good-bye, Baby Sister. Tonight I shall read you my lessons so you can enjoy school with me." With that, Sung ran out of the house and raced with his friends over the dusty trail that led to the schoolhouse. He soon forgot all about the airplanes and the bombs. He had to study hard if he was to make good marks.

Halfway through the afternoon the jets once again came over the village. This was so common that the students usually paid little attention, but this time something was different. The jets circled the village and suddenly dived low over the houses. The first bomb crashed into a cluster of huts some distance from the school with such a terrible explosion that tile slid from the school roof. For awhile the students sat in stunned terror, and then they began to scream. Where could they go? What could they do?

The planes made dive after dive over the village. Sometimes a bomb landed in the rice field sending up huge geysers of water and mud, but usually they landed among the huts, throwing wood and thatch into the air and bursting into huge balls of fire. After a seeming eternity, the great silver birds screamed away and no more bombs fell.

Dust and smoke hung in the air as Sung looked in the direction of his home. Suddenly panic seized him as he began to realize what had happened. The grove of trees that had once surrounded his home was gone. Huge clouds of smoke rose from the crumpled remains of the houses. In terror Sung began to race along the path toward his house. His screams were drowned by those of many other people as they, too, ran hysterically in search of their families.

The next day the bodies of Sung's mother, father, grandmother, and sister were buried in hastily dug graves alongside their ancestors. Sung wept bitterly. He was alone and frightened. There was not time to perform all the necessary rituals, for the people must leave the village and go to a safer place. Perhaps the jets would come again. If he could not perform all of the prayers, the spirits of his parents would be unhappy. Yet he only had time to place burning incense on their graves and then he had to leave. He had to leave the land of his ancestors, the graves of his family.

II.

The sun fought desperately to break through the thick gathering clouds, but it did so vainly. The rain began to fall and soon the city of Saigon was engulfed in a torrential downpour. Sung crowded further back into his little shelter. The cardboard he had fashioned for a roof would keep the rain out this time, but the rainy season had just begun and in time the cardboard would give way and he would have to dig through more trash heaps looking for something suitable for his little shelter.

He was cold and lonely. The city frightened him, but he had no other place to go. He had constructed his small hut down a narrow street near the market. It was just big enough for him to crawl into and lie down. In one corner he had constructed a small altar. On a piece of paper he had drawn small pictures of his parents and sister. Before these he would place burning incense when he could get it. He hoped their spirits would not be unhappy, but he did the best he could and offered prayers to them every day.

Suddenly the sun broke through the clouds and the rain moved on its way. Sung crawled out of his little hut and shivered. He was hungry now and must go find something to eat. He had been in Saigon long enough to know where to beg, but he still did not like begging. He longed to be back on his farm with his family.

"Please give me some piasters for food," he said to a passing Vietnamese. The man reached into his pocket and unconsciously gave Sung a few coins.

"Thank you, sir," he said, as he moved on down the street.

Many of the people simply ignored him as he held out his pleading hand. Others offered him a few piasters or even some of their food. In one day he could usually beg enough money to buy some bread to eat and some incense for his littler altar.

"Please, sir, I'm hungry. Can you help me?"

"Get lost, brat!" The words were strange and angry.

"Please, sir, I'm very hungry."

"I'm giving you nothing, you damn little thief!" The foreigner yelled at Sung in words he could not understand, and struck him across the face. Sung recoiled in terror. He burst into tears and ran as fast as he could from the tall, light-skinned giant. He could not understand that reaction at all. It was obvious that the stranger was rich. He had nice clothes and a camera. Surely he could spare a few piasters.

For days Sung tried to avoid the big foreigners. Their strange vulgar language frightened him, and his face was sore where he had been struck. Yet there were so many of the foreigners on the streets and they seemed so rich; surely they could help him. Gathering courage he tried again to approach them. Putting on his most sorrowful look, he tried again and again. Sometimes they completely ignored him; sometimes they gave him a little money; and other times they cursed at him in their strange language and threatened to hit him. Sung learned to keep alert and ready. But more than that he learned to hate the foreigners, for they were the people who had destroyed his home and his family.

III.

The setting sun cast a red glow over the sky. City lights began to flash their message to all the night visitors. Sung strolled the streets now with assurance. He had grown up in the past years. He was no longer the little beggar kid with the dirty nose and frightened eyes. A tall good looking youth, he wore flared trousers and a trim white shirt. His costume was completed with a pair of sunglasses which he wore night and day.

"Want to change money, sir? I buy dollars for 500 piasters. How about a girl? I know a real nice girl. She friendly and educated. Come with me."

Sung had learned some of the strange language, not much, but enough. He was no longer afraid of the big foreigners. He placed his arm around the man's shoulders and led him in the direction of a bar.

"No I don't want a girl."

"She's nice, real nice. She's friendly and educated."

"Bug off, kid, before I belt ya. I don't want any girl you can take me to. I know your tricks."

"OK, sir." Sung slipped his arm off the shoulder of the man and moved away.

"You're number ten!" he called to the foreigner, as though to get in the final punch.

When Sung turned the corner he lifted his sun glasses and opened the foreigner's wallet.

"So you know my tricks," he thought. "Well this trick was worthwhile to me. I am now ten thousands piasters richer and you are without your papers."

Sung stood on the corner watching the people walk by. There were many girls leaning on the arms of the big foreigners. Those girls were there for the same reason he was. They had been driven from their homes by the war and now had to survive somehow. Like Sung, they were young. They walked along with the foreigners, laughing and talking in the strange language with the few words they knew. They were out to earn money too, and before the evening was over they would have succeeded in collecting from the foreigner in one way or another.

As curfew time approached Sung headed for his small house. He had long since moved out of his cardboard hut and into a more substantial shelter. The little altar he had so carefully taken care of had been left behind. He could only vaguely remember his old home and the traditions of his family. He no longer felt a longing to return. He had been thrust into a new life and the past was being forgotten.

IV.

The sun shone drearily through the curtain of automobile fumes and dust. Sung was riding on the back of a Honda with one of his friends. They were weaving in and out of the traffic looking for unwary victims.

"Get those glasses." Sung's friend advised as he drove his Honda near a car which was stopped at a red light. They sat waiting for the light to change without showing any interest in the lady sitting in the car beside them. Suddenly, as the light changed to green, Sung reached in the open car window, and snatched the glasses from the lady's face. The Honda was down the street before the lady had time to realize what had happened.

That was the second catch of the day. The first had beem a watch from the arm of a Honda driver. Taking something from someone on a Honda was tricky because the Honda drivers often gave chase. But Sung and his friend were willing to take chances, which most Honda drivers were not. They could weave in and out of traffic with only inches to spare and come out laughing. Stealing from cars was even less risky because a car could not go as many places as a Honda could and consequently, escape was easier.

"How about that watch there?"

"No, It's a cheap Japanese make. No need to spend our gas on that one."

"Man, look at that one that soldier in the jeep is wearing. That one must be worth a fortune. Grab it!"

The Honda moved up to the jeep with practiced precision. At the proper moment, Sung reached in, grabbed the watch and twisted it. The band snapped in two and the watch was free. The Honda shot forward. But this time luck was not with them. Traffic on the street was thin and the jeep took off in pursuit. Having few other cars in the street to use as shields, the Honda tried

17

desperately to escape by speed alone. Sung was suddenly aware of the explosive sound of a gun and a sharp piercing pain in his back.

Suddenly, reality returned to Sung as someone reached down and snatched a watch from his clutching fist. He uttered a cry of pain as his body was jerked, but no one offered him aid. The rays of sunlight caressing his unblinking eyes, slowly faded away.

1973

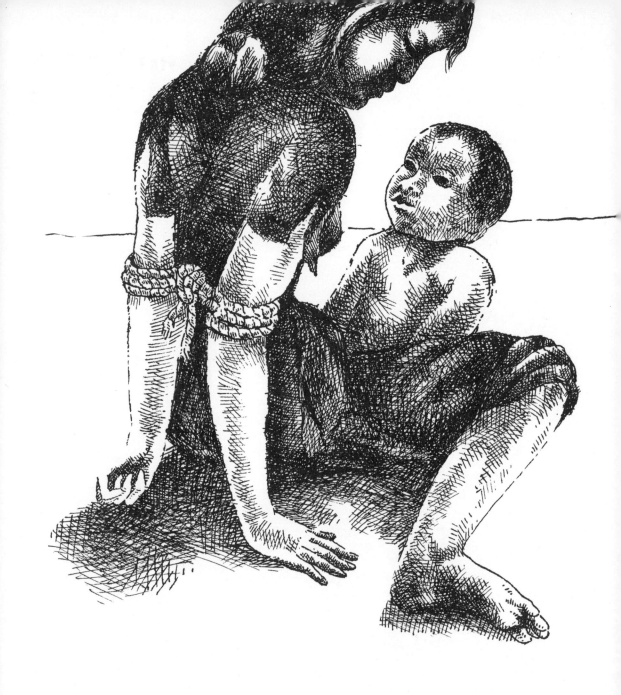

A Christmas Message From the Third World

Narrator: *(Reading from the Bible):* "And thou, child, shalt be called the prophet of the Highest: for thou shalt go before the face of the Lord to prepare his ways; To give knowledge of salvation unto his people by the remission of their sins, Through the tender mercy of our God; whereby the dayspring from on high hath visited us, To give light to them that sit in darkness and in the shadow of death, to guide our feet into the way of peace" (Lk. 1:76-79, KJV).

(Looking up) I guess you are all wondering why I am sitting here reading and meditating instead of enjoying the Christmas feast over in the next room. I must say, I really would like to join them. It certainly smells good. You may think a fast is no way to spend Christmas day, but I had a rather strange experience the other night and that experience has led me to do what I am doing now.

It was really a strange dream. Perhaps my mind was stimulated by all the things I have been reading in the paper lately. There seems to be nothing but bad news these days. But whatever caused it, it was so real that I feel I really met the people I saw in my dream. I saw people in conversation. Some of the people could have been me, or you, or any of our friends here in our neighborhood. The others were strangers. I think they would be called people from the third world. Their conversations went something like this . . .

Scene I

First World: And a merry Christmas to you, my good friend! How are you this beautiful Christmas season?
Third World: Do you want the standard answer, or do you want the truth?
First: There is nothing I admire more in a person than truth. You can feel free to share with me your most honest feelings.
Third: All right, then, to be honest, I'm really not feeling too well this Christmas season. Stomach pains, you know.
First: Oh, yes. I know just how you feel. I just came from my own family Christmas dinner. Great food, really great. That's one of the beautiful things about Christmas. Families getting together and sharing a meal. We had one of the biggest turkeys we could find this year. And the stuffing was terrific!
Third: Sounds good.
First: Be careful, you're drooling. I start drooling too when I think about those

candied sweet potatoes, gravies, buttered buns, and desserts. Why, we had three kinds of pie, including butter pecan—my favorite—two big cakes, and at least four Jello salads.

Third: Sounds quite filling.

First: Filling is hardly the word for it. We ate more than is healthy. But after all, it is Christmas. . . . Yeah, we're all a little upset in the stomach today. Even our two dogs got more than they could eat.

Third: That's too bad.

First: Well, thank goodness for Alkaseltzer. *(Pause)* Yeah, I know what you mean about stomach pains. We experience them every Christmas. By the way, what did you have for dinner? I'll bet you can't surpass the feast we had.

Third: Well, you're right on that point. Actually, we didn't have Christmas dinner. As I was going to say before, our stomach pains are due to hunger. You know, we haven't eaten for three days. This last year our homes were destroyed and our land ruined. Our crops just couldn't grow. To top it off, we were forced to move from our old homes into camps where we couldn't farm. The price of food just doubled and there are no jobs available.

First: Say, that's too bad! Why did you have such bad luck?

Third: I don't know. I really don't understand it clearly. It has something to do with lack of enough resources to go around and power struggles.

First: That really is too bad. Some people just can't think of anyone but themselves. Sorry to hear your Christmas won't be all that happy. Luckily it's the spirit of the thing that counts, isn't it!

Third: I suppose so. But it is hard to have a good spirit when your kids are starving.

First: Say, maybe I can help out a bit. We had a little food left over from Christmas dinner, I'll try to scrape some of it together and send it to you.

Third: You're too kind.

First: Oh, think nothing of it. After all, Christmas is a time of sharing. Anything to help make your Christmas more meaningful.

Third: For the first time in my life I really see what Christmas is all about. Your concern and understanding simply amaze me. Thanks for your table scraps . . . er . . . food, but you may keep them. Your dogs can probably eat more.

First: Well! You don't have to get sarcastic. I was only trying to help.

Third: Your goodwill is misplaced; your eyes are blinded by your wealth. I wish you and your family a very merry Christmas. And do try to forget our situation. I wouldn't want to spoil your Christmas.

First: Oh, don't worry about that. At Christmas time we must think of others. I'm sorry, but I must be going. I promised my kids we would open our gifts this evening. I want to see the looks on their faces when they see the new "speak, walk, and wet" doll and the electric train I bought them. Merry Christmas to you!

Scene II

Person A: Say, tell me, how do you Christians celebrate Christmas?

Person B: Well, Christmas is the celebration of Christ's birthday. If you like, I can read you the story. It's a very interesting one.

A: Oh, I know the story. I've read it many times. We third worlders are curious. We like to know what makes you tick. We can learn a lot about you by your religion. Yes, I have read the story of Christmas. In fact, I have read all of the New Testament. It is very interesting. Sometimes I have even been tempted to see some truth in it; yet I can't see that it has a very positive effect on most of your people.

B: You may have a point there, but you must remember that any religion should be looked at through its teachings, not through the people who attempt to follow that religion.

A: There is truth in what you say, but if the Jesus Christ spoken of in your Christmas story does not affect your people positively, then I must wonder if He is any more powerful or true than the other religious leaders of the world.

B: How do *you* view Christianity?

A: Are you sure you want to ask that question? It makes you vulnerable to criticism.

B: I am willing to listen. Shoot away.

A: As I said, I find the Christmas story most fascinating. It is a beautiful story, and can easily speak to us in the third world, because we can relate easily to a person born in a situation similar to ours. We find it easy to trust someone of our social standing who is wise. However, I think you Christians only leave Christ in the manger long enough to sing your Christmas carols, and then you want to see him on the cross again.

B: What do you mean by that?

A: You have Santa Claus to be the goody-goody person of Christmas. You seem to rather want Christ on the cross. You Christians act as though the rest of the world is responsible for killing your Christ and you have to take revenge.

B: I don't think I quite follow that.

A: All right, let me give you an example. Look at my country. It has been all but totally ruined by your country. Your planes have bombed, strafed, and sprayed our countryside. Thousands of our people have been killed. Our economy is ruined and our life is disrupted. This has been done by your country, run by Christians, and with money supplied by you Christians. You say that you want to preserve our freedom so we can worship and live as we please. What you actually mean is that you want this country safe for your Christian religion and that that religion cannot survive unless your own kind of political and social life is established here. We have in essence killed your

23

Christ, and He can only come down off the cross after you have made it safe for Him here.

B: You sound bitter.

A: I am bitter. I hear your good stories, but I see the facts of my country and its mutilated body. I also see your military. It is the biggest in the world. You control weapons which can destroy all of us in an instant. You police the world, and force your wishes on my government. And then say you have total faith in a God of love and peace.

B: But I am an individual. I cannot be responsible for what my country does.

A: Can you honestly tell me that you have no part in this horrible military machine, that you can take no responsibility for what your country's policies are, and that you have paid *no* money for this war?

B: I cannot deny having some part in all this. Do you hate me for that?

A: I do not hate you for doing what your country asks you to do. You are a citizen of that country and must follow it. But I cannot understand you as a Christian, celebrating this Christmas season and being able to speak about the "Prince of peace" and "joy to the world." If the Christmas story is more than just a story, where does it become real for me to see? When does it become something more than the religion which my people now follow? That is what I want to know when I ask about Christmas in your country. Don't *tell* me about Christmas, *show* me Christmas.

Scene III

Christian: (humming a Christmas carol)

Prisoner: What's the big occasion to make you so happy?

Christian: Oh! You startled me. Why, it's Christmas, didn't you . . . Say! what are you doing in that cage? Is this some kind of a psychology experiment or something?

Prisoner: I guess you might call it that. This is a tiger cage, and they are trying to see how long it takes to force me to say what they want to hear.

Christian: It's a mighty small cage, isn't it? I mean, surely they don't keep you in here for long.

Prisoner: Only about twenty-four hours a day seven days a week. I'm let out for torture occasionally, but I'm not certain I like that better than being penned up in here. I thought you'd like this cage. After all, you built it.

Christian: I built it! What do you mean by that? I may have heard about these things, but I certainly never built one.

Prisoner: Well, let's say your money made it possible.

Christian: You seem awfully young to be penned up in here. How long do you think you'll have to stay?

Prisoner: I've been here for two years already and have no idea how much longer. I've never been tried, you see. Anyway, if I could get out I don't think I would have much of a future. After two years in here I can't walk. That happens easily when one is continually beaten and never allowed to use one's legs.

Christian: Well, as they say, crime doesn't pay.

Prisoner: I was only eighteen when I was arrested. The police came into my house one morning. Before noon I was being interrogated. You have no idea what that can be like. Bright lights in the face that cause the skin to burn, soapy water forced into your stomach, electric shocks—the works. Is there any reason why I shouldn't have become rather cynical and bitter in the past two years?

Christian: Wow! You must have really done something to receive that kind of treatment. What did you do? Rob a bank? Kill someone? Maybe you're one of those mass murderers!

Prisoner: If you really want to know my crime, I'll tell you, but I guarantee you, you won't believe it.

Christian: Oh, it can't be that bad. Go ahead, tell me.

Prisoner: All right, I sang a song about peace.

Christian: Come on now, you don't expect me to . . . .

Prisoner: No, I knew you wouldn't believe it. It's true, but you could never let yourself believe it. After all, you helped pay for this cage and you *have* to believe that it is being used for a good purpose.

Christian: You make us sound so bad. Maybe you are being truthful, I don't know. But even so I don't like to see fellow humans being treated like this. I really would like to help. Especially during this Christmas time.

Prisoner: You really mean that! You really want to help?

Christian: Sure. What can I do?

Prisoner: Why not join me in here. People couldn't avoid noticing if *you* were here. They would have to believe what they hear if they heard it from you. If you really want to empathize with me, then join me.

Christian: Well, I don't know about that. I'm not so certain a Christian should be in prison. We're supposed to live good lives, you know. I was thinking more of collecting some money from my brothers and sisters to share with you. It could buy some food and medicine for you.

Prisoner: Well, why not? You built these things, you might as well try to keep us happy in them. To tell the truth, I could use a little more food. But what I really want is my freedom. You are going to celebrate Christmas this year as you always do. I also want to be with my family. We were very happy and close. Can't you do something to get me out of here?

Christian: Well, here's some money. I really would like you to take it.

Prisoner: All right. I'll take it. Now you can go home to your family and enjoy the celebration. In a few minutes you will forget me. The money you gave me will help you forget.

Christian: I don't know. I really can't see getting myself put in prison. Surely that's not my Christian duty.

Narrator: Well, that was my dream. It was strange, wasn't it? Needless to say, I didn't sleep much the rest of the night. I kept thinking about *this* Christmas season and what it really means to other people.

No, I'm not fasting because I feel guilty about eating so much food today when others have so little. I realize that if I don't eat today, the food prepared for me will not be given to the hungry. I am fasting because I want to spend this time in prayer and study. Christ is speaking to me about Christmas in a new way. I am guilty of creating many of the situations these people find themselves in. As I realize this, I see how my life can be improved. It is as if the Christmas story is coming to life once again. Christ is becoming alive in my life. I am becoming free.

Why don't you join me? As a family, this Christmas, fast together and meditate on the real Christmas. Together we can show the world that it is not the lack of money which is hurting these people, but rather our attitudes, and as we change our attitudes, they will see Christ even before we have had an opportunity to preach to them. Christmas is for the third world. Let's share it with them.

This is a story, and like all good stories it begins, "Once upon a time . . ." But it is not necessarily an old story, for in fact it can be a present-day story. The names and the places have been changed so as not to embarrass anyone, but you may feel free to try to guess who the real characters are and where the story actually takes place. Perhaps that will make it more meaningful to you.

MENNONITE CENTRAL COMMITTEE (CANADA)
201 - 1483 PEMBINA HWY.
WINNIPEG, MANITOBA
R3T 2C8

The Beginning

Once upon a time there was a farmer named John. John lived on a small farm in the land of Usa, and like all of the other farmers in his neighborhood, he worked very hard and loved his farm dearly. He raised some corn and wheat, and had several cows, pigs, chickens and ducks. He wasn't rich, but he did have enough to eat and sometimes he even had enough extra money to buy something nice for his house. John was happy on his farm and he was happy with his life.

Also in the land of Usa was a rich ruler. This man was not a cruel man, but he did demand taxes from all of the small farmers like John. The farmers didn't mind paying these taxes, however, because in return the ruler helped them keep their roads repaired, gave them a fairly good price for their produce, and when their crops failed he would often give them food to eat until their next crop came along. It seemed to be a very good arrangement.

Every month, John and the other farmers would gather their eggs, milk, corn, and wheat together to take to the market. Because the market was usually good, John could quickly sell his produce. Usually he could make one hundred mon each month. When he had completed his selling, he would go to the rich ruler and give him twenty-five mon for his monthly taxes. With the remaining seventy-five mon he would buy his supplies for the next month. When he returned to his house he usually had about twenty-five mon left which he would use for his children's education and other monthly expenses. Although this life was not the easiest, John and the other farmers didn't complain much because they did have food to eat and they were busy.

The land of Usa was divided from the neighboring country by a river. This neighboring country was very different because the people there did not believe in farming. John could sometimes see some of these people across the river, and although he had never met any of them, he thought that they looked quite human. However, he was a little skeptical about people who didn't believe in farming, (after all how can anyone really be happy if he isn't a farmer), but that was their business and not his.

27

The ruler of Usa felt differently. He was convinced that there was something dangerous about people who did not farm; and furthermore, he was convinced that the people really did want to farm but someone was forcing them not to. To be absolutely honest, he also saw all of that land on the other side of the river, and he could not help but think how much more he could offer his own people if he could farm that land.

The rich ruler thought about this seriously for a long time. "Really," he thought, "our neighbors could be so much happier if they were farmers! They are being deprived of their God-given right to make up their own minds, and they are missing an opportunity to make themselves richer. It is really my obligation to help them."

But how could he help? They didn't take kindly to having people tell them the virtues of farming. They just didn't understand.

Finally it occurred to him that the only way he could help them was to destroy their present way of living so they would see how much better it would be if they were farmers. But where would he get the money to take on that project? Why, from the taxes of course. That would mean that he wouldn't have quite enough money to keep the roads in such good condition, and the price for produce might have to go down a little, but his people should be happy to help out such a worthy cause. And anyway, once their neighbors realized the error of their way of living and started farming, everyone would benefit.

So the rich ruler hired men and horses and sent them across the river to help the people there. It was a hard task and an expensive one. It took much more money than the ruler expected.

John was a little unhappy with this new development, and decided to talk to the ruler about it the next time he went to pay his taxes. "How much is this new program costing me?" asked John. "And is it really necessary?"

"Each month you pay me twenty-five mon," said the ruler. "I must use eighteen of those mon to carry on my new development program. This new program is a very short-term program and will soon be over. Then perhaps I will only ask you to pay twenty mon per month. It is best for all of us. Besides, if we do not convince these people to be farmers, they may even corrupt us and ruin our farming life. We must help them, and we must protect ourselves."

John wasn't sure if he understood all of that, but it sounded good, and the ruler said it would last for only a short time. Besides, he *was* the ruler, wasn't he?

As John worked in his fields or took care of his pigs and cows, he could occasionally see clouds of smoke rising from across the river. Sometimes stories would filter back about how homes were being burned and people were being moved into smaller and smaller areas. Some people even said that there was starvation and disease among their neighbors, and that this new program might last for a long time yet.

John had never hated these people even though they were not farmers. He thought they might be good even though they didn't believe in tilling the land. The more he heard about their new problem the more concerned he became. He knew he had to do something. After much thought, John decided that he would have to share some of his food with them. After all, he had enough to eat with a little left over each month, so why not give them a little of it. That seemed like the only thing to do.

The next month, John went to market as usual to sell his produce. He paid his twenty-five mon to the ruler, eighteen of which would be used in the new development program. He bought his own supplies and then he spent five mon more on supplies for his neighbors. It made him feel good that he would be helping them. On this day he returned home with only twenty mon extra.

John sent the extra supplies along with some of his old and discarded clothing across the river. "What a wonderful feeling to know that you are helping others," John thought and went happily back to his farming.

Month after month this life continued. John supplied eighteen mon to the ruler to continue his "development program" (which some radicals were now calling a "destructive program") and John would send five mon worth of supplies plus some of his discarded clothing to help his neighbors. Month after month John watched the clouds of smoke rising across the river, and month after month he listened to the stories of how bad things were there. The short "development program" seemed to have no end.

John became more and more discouraged about the situation. His roads were badly in need of repair and the prices for his produce had not gone up as promised. When would things be back to normal?

"I can't understand why this program goes on and on," thought John, "I wish there were something I could do to make it stop."

And John continued to supply eighteen mon each month to keep the program going, and five mon each month to help his neighbors, and the war continued.

And now the story stops, and like all good stories it should finish with, "And they lived happily ever after—the end." But they are not living happily, and it is not the end.

Remember, today is the beginning, tomorrow may be the end.

I Just Want To Go Home

It was a hot, humid, dusty day when my little world exploded. The heat was as oppressive as the crowded, dirty huts, the barbed wire, the narrow paths full of sewer water, and the hopelessness in the refugee camp. How many hundreds of families were receiving a can of milk that day I cannot recall. All I remember is the feeling of futility, looking over the shambles of what served as home for thousands of refugees, and trying to tell myself that even though one can of milk was not very much, it was of some help, and that was all I could do anyway.

That's all I remember, that is, until I met the little girl. I will never forget that. She was about six years old, with a dirty face, tattered clothing, and tangled hair. A white cloth on her head told me that she was in mourning.

She looked at me with her sad eyes, two tears forming to drop noiselessly to her cheeks.

"Uncle, why do you have to give me this milk?"

"Because there's no other way for you to get food."

"Why is that, Uncle?"

"There's no food in refugee camps."

"But Uncle, why do I have to live here?"

"There's a war going on, Little One."

"I like my home so much better. Why can't I go home?"

"The war's going on. There's still bombing there."

"Why are they fighting, Uncle?"

"It's hard to understand, Little One. Most adults don't understand."

"But they dropped bombs on my home."

"I know, Little One. It makes me sad."

"My mother and father are still there."

"Maybe you'll get to see them again soon."

"When, Uncle? When?"

"I don't know, Little One. When the war is over."

"Will it be over soon?"

"I don't know. I hope so."

"I'm sad, Uncle. I don't want to cry any longer."

"I don't want to cry any more either. Do you want this milk?"

"No, I just want to go home."

I looked at her pleading face, and then down at the can of milk. The good-will wilted in the oppressive atmosphere of the refugee camp. My mind raced with questions:

Why *is* the war still going on?

What *more* can I do?

Isn't this can of milk of any value?
And the only answer I could hear was a soft, trembling voice saying, "I just want to go home, Uncle."

The war is over now. Peace has at last come. I imagine the little girl has finally gone back home. She's gone to visit her mother and father and placed fresh wild flowers on their graves.

She has given me a new vision. The helping hand holding out a can of milk has faded away, and in its place is an outstretched hand saying, "How can I help you go home?"

Mother Viet Nam

The old mother sits
by the door of her homeland
waiting the time
when she once more can stand.
She mourns for her son
who has gone to the battle.
With tears in her eyes
she asks of the world:

When will this war end?
When will peace begin?
When will this killing and hatred cease?
When will we forgive?
When will we let live?
When will we love as one big family?

O Mother Viet Nam,
the days have been long for you.
Nothing but war
have your old eyes seen.
Once young, beautiful, you were
full of life and of courage,
now you are broken and battered.
I hear loud your cry:

How will this war end?
How will peace begin?
How will this killing and hatred all cease?
How will we forgive?
How will we let live?
How will we love as one big family?

Your sons are all dead
and your soil has turned red.
The hope for your life
has been drained.
O Mother Viet Nam, how I long to uphold you,
to help you to stand
and to make this command:

Now will this war end.
Now will peace begin.
Now will this killing and hatred all cease.
Now will we forgive.
Now will we let live.
Now will we love as one big family.

1974

There was a great hope among the people in the refugee camps to be able to one day return to their old villages, and once again establish their ties with their traditions. Thuan, a young English student of mine, shared this poem with me as he thought about the day he would be able to return to the land which for so many years had been in his family. I have translated it from the Vietnamese.

My Return

I'll return to my homeland
after days of bloodshed
of massacres and destruction
filled with fears and terror.

I'll return to my Quang Ngai
after days of separation
of pain and sorrow
filled with suffering and desperation.

I'll return to my heritage
composed not only of family and friends
but of Quang Ngai's countryside, and the Tra Khuc River
where I swam every morning.

I'll return and see my village
with its small, peaceful garden,
and visit my old grandmother
who anxiously awaits my returning.

Oh! How wonderful my return is!
Oh! How wonderful my return is!   Thuan

The Spirit of the Soil

Menno stands looking over his field of waving green wheat. In a few weeks he will be able to harvest it and once again his granaries will be full.

He stoops down and takes a handful of the soil in hand. As the dark rich soil runs through his fingers, he experiences a feeling that only a person attached to the soil can know. His grandfather settled this land and broke the sod almost a hundred years ago. It has been in the family since; it will stay in the family.

This wheat crop will be a good one. There should be plenty in the bank this winter to care for the family, even after taxes.

* * * * * *

Nguyen stands at the edge of the refugee camp, gazing across the bare countryside to the edge of the mountains. There, he knows, is rich land. Ten years ago he left that land—land which had belonged to his father, his father's father and to many generations before that.

In those days, ten years ago, Nguyen had not been a rich farmer, but like the others in the village, he had had enough to eat, and with his wife and five children had had a very happy life. He had dearly loved that land. His ancestors were buried there, and he too would find rest in that soil.

However, things did not go so well. Planes had suddenly flown over, dropping leaflets announcing that all villagers were to move immediately. This land was to become a free-fire zone. Nguyen and the other farmers discussed this but decided to stay. This was their land! Their very life! How could they leave?

The next day the planes returned, but instead of dropping leaflets, they dropped bombs. Nguyen had been in the field harvesting his precious rice. The bombs came so suddenly that everyone was caught by surprise. The death toll was high. Nguyen had lost his wife and youngest child in that attack. By evening, foreign soldiers had moved in and all survivors were forced to move. They had not even had time to bury their dead.

Life in the refugee camp had been difficult. There were many days of waiting. Waiting to return home. Waiting for food. Waiting for someone who would listen.

The years dragged on. Still there was no peace. One of Nguyen's neighbors had decided to return home anyway. There was no life in camp; surely he would be able to plant his rice and find some way to live on his old land. But he had been shot immediately. The officials said he was a VC (Viet Cong) because he was in a free-fire zone. Nguyen and his neighbors know that the man had just been going home.

As years passed by, Nguyen had listened to artillery fall on his land by the mountains, had watched planes burn, bombing and spraying his beloved soil, had watched his oldest child slowly die of sickness.

And then had come the hope of the Paris Accords. Peace was coming! They would all be able to go home. Finally they would grow their own rice again. They would build their homes. They would live again!

They moved back as a village. Their excitement was great, but they broke down in tears when they saw the total destruction of their land. Houses were piles of rubble, trees were shredded, craters covered their rich farm lands. It would take much work and many years to repair this. But they would do it. This was home! They belonged here! They had at long last been reunited with their land.

But their rebuilding was short-lived. A few days after their arrival, soldiers threatened and harassed them, and told them to return to the camp. That night artillery came once again. Reluctantly the villagers returned to the camp, carrying their shattered hopes with them. What was this Paris agreement? Why was a promise made only to be broken?

Along with several other villagers, Nguyen decided to return to the old home during the day to farm, and then at night, when the artillery came they would return to the camp. At least they could be busy, and perhaps even grow some rice.

Digging into the soil which had lain untilled for ten years brought strength and joy back to Nguyen. The sun was hot, the soil hard, his throat parched, but Nguyen felt happier than he had for ten years. The smell of freshly turned soil soothed his lungs. Behind him a patch of rich black soil grew as each bite of his hoe turned the sod.

But a new terror soon struck. An explosion in the next field suddenly interrupted the sounds of chopping hoes and happy people. A woman neighbor lay on her freshly turned soil, her body broken and lifeless. Her hoe had struck an unexploded grenade. The hope that this was only a freak accident faded quickly as two more villagers died that day in their fields, and as others found unexploded ordnance lying in their fields.

37

* * * * * *

At night the war goes on, with artillery and bombs. In the day shooting continues and a few villagers go to the fields to try to turn over a little more soil. Every now and then another villager is carried back to the village, a victim of an unwanted and unending war.

Nguyen kneels at the edge of the camp and tears fill his eyes. He may never see his beloved home again. Not because of the dangers, but because his camp is being moved south, to "secure lands" they say. Didn't the Peace Accords say he could go freely anywhere he wanted? Then why is he being forced to move south to a strange and frightening place? Nguyen misses his wife, his youngest child and his oldest child. He misses his second child who has been pulled into the army and now is forced to kill his own people. And Nguyen misses his land, his home, his family altar. Why can't he go home? Why has he been forced to suffer and wait these ten years only to be taken to a different area where his future is empty. He grips a handful of loose sand and his spirit cries out, cries out for his family, for his home, for his land, for peace!

* * * * * *

Menno is slowly rising to his feet, the last bits of black soil falling between his fingers, when the cry reaches him. He stands, listening.

Two men, half a world apart, yet with so much in common. They both love the soil. They love to grow their crops and supply the needs of their families. They both simply desire to live in peace.

Their spirits have touched. The one pleading for help in finding peace, the other capable of helping in that search.

Time pauses in balance. The one with sand running through his fingers, crying out, the other with rich soil clinging to strong hands, hesitating.

One of the drawings Buu Chi slipped out of prison was of hands eagerly reaching up for the dove of peace which was hovering overhead. It reminded me that those who struggle for a nonviolent path to peace are indeed in the minority. Yet, the persistent struggle of a small minority can pave the way to peace and love. The important thing is not to give up.

Peace

In the blinding glare
of darkness
a small light
flutters and
blinks,
seeking to break
the clutch
of darkness.

As it gains support
it breaks
a crack
in the thick gloom,
giving a guiding light
to a small symbol
of hope.

Slowly,
carefully,
the small white
dove
descends,
to rest and
preen
its battered feathers
on the outstretched hands
of those
who call
for peace.

40

1975

42

Bunche 1973 CH. ID

The war ended rather abruptly on 30 April 1975. It was strange to suddenly hear such silence after the savage fighting of the previous days. There was a mixture of intense feelings among people as one era ended and a new, uncertain future began.

30 April 1975

The silence!
Can you hear the silence?
The guns, the planes, the bombs,
all rest and give peace back to the land.
The long nightmare is over.
Blood now flows strongly through young veins,
not over rough and restless soil.
The shout!
Did you hear that shout?
It is the shout of joy
raised from the throats of people at last free.
A new era has begun.

That rumble!
Did you hear that rumble?
The sound of prison walls falling
frees those spirits which for years have struggled to be free.
At long last the prisons are dead,
and hand grasps hand as liberation spreads
bringing together those who were forced foes.
That laughter!
Did you hear that laughter?
It is the sound of youth
raising their voices in song for freedom and peace.
Those who have been imprisoned are now free.

That splintering!
Did you hear that splintering?
It is the yoke of bondage
being shattered by hands that only struggle for peace.
The days of slavery are over;
Viet Nam now belongs to Vietnamese.
And her destiny is in her hands.
That tremble!
Did you feel that tremble?
Millions of rice plants are breaking soil,
bringing new life to a land and a people.
The yoke of dependency rots in the mud.

Return of the Spirit of the Soil

The golden veil of the evening covers the sky as the sun slowly begins to set behind the massive Truong Son Mountains which guard the western edge of the newly opened rice paddies. A cool, soft breeze tenderly caresses away the harsh heat of the day, and in the rustling leaves of the bamboo, a bird begins its song of welcome to the coming of another peaceful night.

With agonizingly slow steps, Nguyen walks to the water well. His rusty and worn hoe rests across his tired naked shoulder, and his body covered with dust and sweat yearns for a rest. He pauses by the well and turns to look once again at the small patch of rich soil which has been turned over today for the first time in ten years. The last rays of the sun sparkle in his happy eyes.

Nguyen stands alone, looking out over the land, but he feels the presence of his beloved wife who died here ten years ago under the reign of bombs. He speaks to her now in his simple and moving way.

"This first day in our field has been a long and hard one. I didn't get as much done as I should. This old body has become reluctant to do hard labor after those ten years of waiting. All during the day it cried out for a rest. Now my muscles jerk in agony with my every move. Here is the old water well. I could sit down here and give my body the rest it so longs for. But let me stand here just a bit longer. Let me enjoy this sharp pain of overworked muscles for just a few minutes more. During the ten years of waiting in the refugee camp I tried to recall this feeling, the weary but happy feeling after a long day of hoeing in the field. Now that I finally feel that pain, I want to enjoy it for as long as I can. Although the pain is great, it is nothing compared to the pain of war and waiting. This pain is the most precious thing I have ever felt.

"In a few months, we will be able to see the results of the pain. There, where now there is only a small patch of freshly turned soil, and a bigger patch of overgrown land, will soon be a field of waving rice like a green restless ocean under the gentle breeze. There will be food to feed us and a new life under a peaceful sky. We've come home! At long last, we've come home!

"And look, our old well is offering its cool liquid to wash this dust and sweat from my body and to refresh my dry, parched throat. I'll wait just a little longer, for this dust and mud is from my mother earth and I want to feel its coarse protection over my body a little longer. Dust is the badge of a person attached to the soil, and I want to wear it with pride. We are one with our soil.

"My throat feels like the desert sands and my eyes sting from the drops of sweat still rolling from my forehead. For so many years I sat in that camp, gazing out to this land and longing to again feel that my throat would never receive enough water and my eyes never be rid of the salt. Now I want to hold on to this feeling for as long as I can. We have at last come home! After ten years of waiting, today is truly our homecoming!"

Nguyen stands there a moment more, his mind overcome with the beauty of his homeland. The final ray of the setting sun is reflected in the tear of joy which runs down his cheek.

* * * * * *

Menno stops his tractor and glances across the vast, flat fields toward the horizon, where the setting sun throws its red fingers across the sky. The air is filled with the aroma of fresh, rich soil. He brushes the day's collection of dust from his arms as though he does not want to lose one precious speck of this life-giving element.

Suddenly, and without warning, a strange lump forms in his throat. Menno feels an urge to stay for just a minute longer to enjoy the fatigue of tired and weary muscles. Somewhere, someone is experiencing an ecstatic joy, and that spirit is calling out to Menno to share in that joy. The last rays of sunlight catch a small unexplained tear in Menno's eye. Can these two spirits, separated by half a world, yet united in one deep love for the soil, ever truly meet and become one family?

On a quiet, rainy afternoon, Tieu stood on the porch of the Mennonite Central office, quietly watching the streams of water run off the trees. She must have been thinking about her land and her people, for suddenly she entered the office and wrote the following poem. It is her dream for the future.

The Rain*

Have you ever
seen such a beautiful sight,
my friend?
On the veranda
of
my second home
she is standing there
quietly,
looking at the silver chain of
the afternoon rain.

Peace
is a strange world
to her beloved country.
Peace,
a bright future
in her wonderful daydream—
peace,
a beautiful image
to the ones who hate war
and death.

Tieu

47

*Both this poem and the one on page 79 were written in English. (Tieu was a student of English literature.) I think she meant the poems for English ears rather than Vietnamese ears. We were a very close group in our office and did many things together. When we foreigners wanted to express something to our Vietnamese friends, we tried to do it in Vietnamese because we felt it was more meaningful and personal. Our Vietnamese co-workers would try to do the same in English. I think it was our way of telling each other that we respected each other's culture, society, and values.

Like a dream
in the street of her hometown
she sees
people walking in the rain,
hand in hand,
shouting:
"Listen to this good news, my friends!
Peace
has come
to our beloved homeland!"

And then,
in that exciting moment,
she sees
through the rain
the blooming of a brand new world,
a very strange world
without
war, tears, hatred
without
prisons, torture, and absurd death.

And then
young lovers
will never be separated.
People
will no more die horrible deaths.
Innocent children
will never be miserable orphans,
nor life be
a hell on earth.

And then
the future generations
will
rebuild their war torn land
into a strong
and prosperous one
by
working diligently
on their ever green land.

Outside
in the winding street
of my hometown,
still fall
the happy tears of the sky;
but
the strange world
in that afternoon rain
is not a dream
anymore.

Still
on the veranda
of
my home
she is standing there,
peacefully
looking at the silver chain of
the afternoon rain.
Isn't it
a beautiful sight, my friend?

On 18 December 1972 the United States launched a bombing attack against North Viet Nam which lasted until December 29. During those twelve days, 100,000 tons of bombs equaling the explosive power of five atomic bombs of the size dropped on Hiroshima, were dropped on Hanoi and Hai Phong. On the third anniversary of that attack I wrote "The Twelve Days of Christmas." Peace is far more than just the end of hostilities. Peace will never be achieved until we can all come together in confession and forgiveness, and seek ways to rebuild that which we have destroyed.

The Twelve Days of Christmas

Once upon a time there were two giants called Aci and Rema. These two giants were huge and strong, and often liked to climb to the top of a big hill and roar.

When they would roar, many of the small people who lived in the meadow below would shake with fright. This made Aci and Rema feel real good.

"We're so strong we can do anything we like," they often said to each other as they stood on the hill and roared.

However, there were some little people in the valley called Vims who seemed to ignore Aci and Rema. When Aci and Rema would roar, these Vims would just continue hoeing their gardens, or sweeping out their houses. Of course this made Aci and Rema angry.

"Those Vims should show us proper respect," Aci said to Rema one day. "I think it's time we teach them a lesson."

So Aci and Rema climbed up on the hill and yelled down to the Vims in the meadow below, "Starting tomorrow, every Vim must leave his work and bow down and tremble when we roar. You have to give us the respect which is our due."

The next morning Aci and Rema climbed back up the hill and looked down on the peaceful meadow where the Vims were busy at work planting their gardens. On the count of three, Aci and Rema let loose one of their most earthshaking roars.

Several of the Vims threw down their hoes in fear and knelt down at the foot of the hill, shaking with fear. However, most of the Vims just kept right on working as though they did not hear Aci and Rema roaring. Of course, this made Aci and Rema even madder.

"We will give you another chance," Rema shouted down to the Vims. "Tomorrow morning we will come to roar again. Make certain that you are prepared to respect us."

The Vims called a meeting. How would they react to this threat? One of the old Vims stood up and said, "We will bow down to no giants. Why should we pay homage to them? Tomorrow let us go back to our fields and work as usual."

The Vims all shook their heads in approval. They had a lot of work to do and couldn't always stop whenever the giants decided to roar.

The next morning Aci and Rema once again took their place on the hill. This time they gave forth an even more ferocious roar. Again several Vims fell down on their knees, trembling, but most of the Vims looked up, smiled a little and went on with their work.

This time Aci and Rema were shaking with anger. "We gave you two chances," Aci yelled down to the Vims. "You have failed to give us proper respect. Tomorrow you must pay the price."

The next day, which was also the start of the Christmas season, the Vims looked up the hill and saw Aci and Rema standing beside a huge pile of very large rocks. Some of the rocks were big enough to smash a Vim house. Others were even big enough to smash a Vim school or a Vim factory.

"You have had your chance," Aci yelled. "You must be punished for your disrespect."

With that Aci and Rema each picked up a huge rock and threw it into the meadow. They kept throwing rocks, smashing Vims' houses, smashing the Vims' schools, hospitals and factories, and even smashing some of the Vims.

But instead of cowering in fear as Aci and Rema had expected, the Vims got angry and started throwing stones back. The Vims were small, and their rocks were small, but sometimes they hit Aci and Rema.

"Ouch!" yelled Rema as a stone bounced off his nose. "What right have they to throw stones at us like that?"

"They're just trying to make trouble," said Aci as he tried unsuccessfully to dodge a stone.

Aci and Rema began throwing stones even harder and faster. Every time they got hit by one of the Vims' stones, they got angrier. Those stones didn't damage Aci and Rema very much physically, but they certainly did hurt their pride.

Aci and Rema kept throwing stones and smashing the Vims' houses, their schools, their factories, their hospitals, and the Vims themselves. But the Vims just would not give up.

Finally, after twelve days, Aci and Rema stopped throwing their stones. Their arms ached, and they had bruises all over their bodies. But even more than that, their pride had suffered a terrible beating.

With their heads bent, and rubbing their bruises, they left the hill and returned to their giant house. But they left a lot of destruction behind them. The once beautiful meadow was now full of ruins, and the gardens were full of

51

huge stones which would make farming almost impossible.

The Vims were excited about their victory, but were saddened when they looked at their meadow.

"We can fix this up," they said to each other. "As difficult as it is going to be, it will not be as difficult as making those two giants get off that hill and stop throwing stones. However, they are responsible for all this destruction, they ought to help us repair it. Let's go talk to them."

So a delegation of Vims went to the house of the giants. Aci and Rema were sitting there in sullen anger, rubbing their sore arms and legs.

"You really did a lot of damage to our homeland," the visiting Vims told Aci and Rema. "We don't want to be enemies with you. We're willing to try to forget the past. However, we would like to ask you to come help repair some of the damage you did to the land of the Vims."

"Vims?" Aci said to Rema. "I've never heard of any Vims. What are they anyway?"

Rema just shook his head and continued to smash flies and ants in sullen anger.

The Vims returned to their meadow and reported to the people what had happened. A meeting was called to discuss this problem. One of the wise old Vims stood up and said, "We may be a small people, but we are determined. We can repair our meadow. We really do not need the help of those two giants to rebuild. However, we would at least like to have a friendly relationship with them. It is not their money which can repair the great damage they have done to our land. The only thing which can really start to repair all the damage is if they recognize their great wrong in trying to destroy us, and come as equals, seeking reconciliation. We can only wait until they are ready to do that. Until then, we have much work to do. We must all head back to the fields and begin the great task before us. We must build our land!"

The Vims gave enthusiastic nods of support, and went out to the meadow to rebuild.

Earl Martin remained with us in Viet Nam for three months after the war's end before returning to America to join his wife and two children. In one of his letters to us, he mentioned that the world cannot understand those who would risk walking through mine fields in order to plant flowers. That statement reminded me of how Christ chose to "plant flowers" of love and forgiveness among a world that hated Him and finally killed Him.

You Will Reap What You Sow

In the central plains of South Viet Nam, there is a beautiful valley lying between the massive Truong Son Mountains on the west, and the South China Sea on the east. In the center of this valley, lying peacefully amongst the emerald green rice fields, a small hill raises its bare back to the hot summer sun. The hill contains no foliage, and its red soil stands out sharply against the green rice fields, a constant reminder of a not so peaceful history.

Down a narrow dusty path which winds from the bamboo encircled village, through these green rice fields, on past the bare red hill, and into the western mountains, a man was trudging. He was stooped, and appeared old, but his step was light and his muscles young and strong. His eyes were vacant as though they belonged to a madman, but upon closer investigation one could see in their depths a fire burning, as though from a vision—a hope for the future.

Across one shoulder he was balancing a pole with two baskets suspended from the ends. The baskets were filled with young seedling plants. In one hand he carried a hoe and with the other he balanced the shoulder pole while the two baskets swung in rhythm to his steady steps. Sometimes soft music escaped from his lips, but most of the time he appeared to be lost in a world of his own.

So deep in his meditations was he that he failed to notice another figure approaching from the opposite direction. They would have collided on the narrow path had not the stranger called out, "Oh ho, my friend! Let's take caution in passing on this narrow path so one of us doesn't accidently land in the mud of this rice paddy."

The man tried to arrest his steps at the sound of the stranger's voice, but the momentum of the baskets carried him forward a few steps more.

"I'm sorry to frighten you," the stranger laughed. "This path is too narrow to pass on without caution. Where are you heading with those baskets and a mind so far removed from our existence?"

Without answering, the man pointed with his left hand to the small hill which was shimmering in the waves of the summer heat. The stranger's eyes slowly followed the man's extended hand until his eyes came to rest on the hill. With a sudden start he looked back at the man.

"You can't go there!" the stranger cried. "Don't you know that hill is covered with mines? Nobody can go on that hill without getting blown to pieces."

Without looking at the stranger, the man answered, a small smile of determination playing around his lips, "I must go there. I have a very important duty to fulfill on that hill. I must go!"

At this the stranger laughed. Surely this man carrying the baskets was deranged. He was not one to be taken seriously. "And just what do you have to do on that hill that's so important?" he asked.

At this the man looked at his baskets. His voice was filled with feeling. "I'm going to plant these flowers on that hill."

The stranger's laughter broke the stillness of the afternoon. He looked down at the man, humor mixed with pity in his eyes. "Now look my friend, why don't you turn around and walk back with me to your village. It's too hot to be out now anyway."

The stranger put his hand on the man's shoulder as though to turn him around. With a sudden shrug, the man brushed the stranger's hand off his shoulder and tried to push his way past.

"No! I must go to the hill. I must plant these flowers on that hill!"

The stranger stepped back, startled by this sudden outburst from a man who seemed so meek. Again he put his hand on the man's shoulder and this time he pleaded, "Don't go to that hill, I beg you. It's covered with instant death. I've seen those things go off. I've heard the screams of pain and carried the shattered bodies away from that hill. I've seen innocent children blown instantly to pieces. I know what I'm talking about."

54

For the first time the man looked directly into the eyes of the stranger and saw a fire which he had not noticed before. The man spoke in a voice which frightened, yes almost terrorized the stranger.

"And I, I have seen the power of flowers. I have seen them change the hate in people's eyes into looks of love. I have seen them bring back together those who were separated. I have seen them make beautiful, that which is ugly. They have transformed many barren, death-infested hills into gardens where young lovers can meet, and where the lonely can talk with their God. The roots of the flowers sink deep into the soil, pushing their small arms into the devices of destruction, breaking them apart and taking from them their ability to destroy. Yes, I have seen the power of flowers and I am going to plant these flowers in that mine field."

With that he stepped past the stranger. The stranger made a move as though to stop him once again, but something held him back. "He's crazy. He's a deranged fool," the stranger said to himself in awe as he watched the man, baskets swinging happily, begin the assent of the hill of death.

Shortly after the war ended I saw a movie about the life of Nguyen van Troi, a young worker who protested against the war and the American presence in his country. He was arrested, charged with being a Communist and consequently killed. After viewing the film, I thought back to an event which happened shortly after my arrival in Viet Nam in 1971. At that time, another Nguyen, Nguyen Thai Binh was studying in America under a government scholarship. He was very active in the antiwar movement, and I guess this was an embarrassment to both the U.S. and the Vietnamese governments. His visa was revoked and he was forced to return to Viet Nam. He protested his return because he said his life would be in jeopardy. Still he was forced to go, and according to reports, he tried to hi-jack the 747 to Ha Noi. After the plane landed in Saigon, the pilot came to the back of the plane and overpowered Nguyen. Obviously unarmed, Nguyen made no attempt to fight back. The pilot began strangling him and then yelled for a passenger in the plane who just happened to have a gun to "shoot the s.o.b." Nguyen was shot six times and then thrown out of the plane window. Later in an interview, the pilot said he had prayed that God would help him handle the situation, and he gave the thanks to God. These kinds of experiences "radicalized" my thinking very much, and caused me to write "The Final Judgment."

The Final Judgment

On a hot, stifling October day
a young man stands alone,
looking for the last time
at his beloved Viet Nam.
His shout for freedom
is drowned by the muskets of vengeance—
but not before that shout
echoes through the streets of Saigon
and reverberates around the world.
He sags forward,
his life flowing from open wounds
to color red the land of his birth.

Who killed Nguyen van Troi?
Who dared to pass the judgment
which took his life from this world?

"Not I,"
said the judge.
"I only obey the laws."
"And I must follow orders,"
said the arresting officer.
"And it was not my bullet,"
said the executing soldiers.
"I was only protecting the interests of the Vietnamese,"
said the American advisor.
"And I,"
said the man who made the guns,
"was only trying to feed my family."

But the rest of the American people
remain silent,
and the final judgment awaits.

The hot July sun
makes a steamy mist
around the 747.
In the bowels
of the Pan Am giant
the sounds of vengeance are again heard.
A body is spewed violently from the door
and drops lifelessly to the ground.
Is it possible that a human being is treated so—
thrown about like a sack of used clothing,
cast aside as having no value?
How can it be possible, as the
assailant claimed
that God decreed the act?

Who killed Nguyen Thai Binh?
Who bears the responsibility for destroying
this son of Viet Nam?

"Not I,"
said the pilot,
"I had to protect my plane."
"Nor I,"
said the state department official.
"I had to protect American interests."

"And I shot in self-defense,"
said the policeman.
"I," said the bullet maker,
"had to feed my family."
And the rest of America
remains silent.
The final judgment awaits.

The sun warms the dew-covered valley.
A wisp of fog hovers gently.
The flowers sway in the smiling breeze.
The final judgment is being made.
Who killed Nguyen van Troi?
Who killed Nguyen Thai Binh?
The judge, policeman, and advisor,
the soldier, pilot, and state department official,
the bullet maker and the gun maker,
all stand silently.
It is not really they who are on trial,
for their many excuses
describe their guilt.
It is those who have remained silent
who must now answer the question,
"Why?
"Why do you remain silent
while others die?
"Why do you remain silent
while suffering and oppression continue?"
The silence is deafening.

A voice rumbles over the silence
"How many more deaths?
How many more wars?
How much longer will the blood flow
and lifeless bodies fall
before you break your silence?"

*Tin's brother was a young draftee in the South Vietnamese army. In early 1975
he received a serious stomach wound and during the next few months he
remained in the hospital, unable to make any progress. Several months after
the war ended, his wound finally proved fatal and he became another statistic
of the war. How senseless his death was! I could not help but think that if the
war had just ended several months sooner, he would have escaped it
unharmed and be alive today to help his family in their rice fields.*

The Bird and the Storm

The storm terrorized the countryside.
Dark clouds swirled madly through the sky.
The wind beat against the trees and hills
while thunder shook the air and crashed about.

He stood with face pressed against the window,
his eyes glued to a tree in which a small bird perched.
He watched the valiant struggle to survive the storm,
hoping against hope the sun would shine soon.

The small bird fluttered its wings to hold its perch
as the wind tossed the tree about.
Rain beat upon its feathers
threatening to wash it to the ground.

"Hold on little bird!"
he shouted above the roaring thunder.
"Just a little longer and the storm will be over.
Don't give up your struggle yet."

Lightning flashed and the tree lurched in the wind.
The small bird began to fall, but one small foot held on.
With weak but determined wings
it once again regained its perch.

The storm began to pass, then came again.
With each crash of thunder and each gust of wind
he was certain the little bird would fall.
But the bird, though small, was courageous.

Suddenly the dark clouds parted and the sun broke through.
"You're safe! You're safe!" he called triumphantly.
But then his shout turned to a cry of alarm,
for the small bird toppled limply to the ground.

He rushed outside to cradle it in his small hands.
Vainly it tried to flutter its wings.
He tenderly held it up to the sun
so the warm rays could soothe the battered feathers.

"The storm's over," he said softly.
"It's quiet and beautiful now.
All the other birds are rejoicing,
why can't you join them?"

But the little bird's eyes were closed.
It could not see the bright spring flowers.
It could not feel the warm sun,
nor could it hear the happy songs of the other birds.

"The storm's over," he said, tears burning his eyes.
"You can fly about freely with the other birds now.
You survived the storm.
Why can't you enjoy the peace?"

He held the little bird above his head.
"Fly! Fly!" he pleaded.
"Fly about with the other birds.
You're free now. Fly!"

But the little bird
who had struggled so hard to survive,
now lay still and silent in his small hands.
Never again would it fly.

New experiences are frightening. We are afraid of the risks of entering a situation in which there are so many uncertainties and unknowns. But it is those who are willing to take risks who are finally able to make a real difference in the world.

Like a Dream

Like a dream
the rain-washed street
reflects the soft glow of street lights.
The night is without sound,
without sight.

In ao ba ba,*
black hair falling over shoulders,
she is at home here.

The murmur of the mind
reflects on the scene:

She
is alone on the street,
her friends having taken
other streets.
She,
afraid of the silent
cave of darkness,
determined to continue on.

She takes this street,
for truly it is her street,
and without her
it would be even more dark
and lonely.

61

*the *ao ba ba* consists of loose slacks and shirt, and is the costume worn by Vietnamese farmers.

Slowly she passes
under the street light,
and is folded into the darkness.
What awaits her
at the street's end?

This moment is sad,
it is memorable,
it is poetic.
Because of those who
dare move down such streets,
even though fearful and hesitant,
there will be a dawn,
and a new beauty.

The World Market

"What kind of world do you want, brother?"
"What kind of world do you want, sister?"
"Special price for you!"
"Buy here!"
"Buy here!"

As I stood in the midst of the world market,
the confusing sounds and sights battered me about.
How do you find the kind of world you want
from all this confusion?

"I have just the world for you!"
a seller called.
"Buy from me and you shall be satisfied.
I guarantee my worlds."

I stop and look around.
Everyone is calling out their wares,
convincing others that their world
is the best.
How can I choose?

"Buy your world here!"
The seller has a hard voice.
"I specialize in violence.
Just a little violence
to break the monotony?
Or, perhaps, a world
with a big war?
Do you want guns?
   or knives?
      or bombs?
         or stones?
            or clubs?
               or words?
                  or looks?
                     or thoughts?
I have all kinds.
Buy your violent world here!"

63

In utter dismay,
I look at his display.
It is bloody and mangled.
There is a look of sadistic delight in his eyes.
"Have you no world of peace?"
I ask innocently.

"Peace?"
He says the word with a sneer.
"You don't get peace from a violent world.
You get more violence.
We design them that way.
If it's peace you want,
go down this alley."

I avoid his mocking look
and hurry down the alley.
Again the sounds surround me.

"Buy from me!
The best in hungry worlds.
We have severe famines,
   overpopulation
      pestilence
         disease
            misuse
               hoarding
                  selfishness
                     luxury
                        overeating.
You can't buy a better hungry world.
Starvation is guaranteed!"

The display case is enormous.
One corner is fat,
the rest is thin and hungry.

"Don't you have a world
in which all are satisfactorily fed?"
I ask, my voice quivering.

He looks at me in pity.
"You can't have everyone well fed.
Then there wouldn't be the overfed.
Only when the majority are hungry
can these worlds exist.
Which one will you buy?"

I hurry on,
trying to erase the sights
of that display case.
I move down the narrow
winding market streets,
bumping into others who are
just as confused as I,
struggling as in a dream
to understand all that is around.

"This way! This way!
Oppressive worlds,
today on discount."

I stop to look
without knowing why.
The display case holds chains
   whips
      blank textbooks
       propaganda
         fear
           dependency
           power
             egotism
             walls.

"I have just the world
you're looking for,"
he says, banging the counter with his fist.
"You can be either king or slave,
whichever suits your fancy.
You can rule, and stomp and persecute,
or you can whimper, cower and weep.
Your choice for the best in oppressive worlds.
We guarantee good trade-ins

as new oppressive structures are designed.
You can't lose here!"

"I want to be neither king nor slave,"
I say almost angrily.
"I just want a simple world
in which we can all be happy
and live in love."

He stares at me silently.
I cannot meet his glare.
Finally he speaks
in a condescending voice.
"Your kind of world is not here.
We don't deal in such ridiculous things.
Perhaps the idealist can help you.
You seem more his type."
Try this alley."

One last hope!
The idealist must have the world for me.
I move down the winding streets
asking for directions.
Some people suggest trying
this street or that.
Others simply shake their heads
and shrug their shoulders.
Some laugh and others jeer.
At last I come to a seldom-used path.

Weeds cover it,
and the sign is rusty.

"This surely can't be right,"
I tell myself over and over.
But something compels me to go on.
At the end of the street is a lonely market stall.
There is no display case,
just bits and pieces lying around.

The proprietor has a friendly
but distant look.

"I'm looking for a world,"
I say.
"I don't want violence
   or hunger
      or hate
         or fear
            or misery.
Can you help me?"

His look slowly surrounds me.
He doesn't look *at* me, but *in* me.
"Have you tried the other stalls?"
His voice is strong.

"I've been searching all day,"
I answer wearily.
"Nothing I see appeals to me.
I have bought nothing."

"Few people come here,"
he says.
"And most of those who do,
go away disappointed.
What makes you think I have the world for you?"

"You are my last hope.
All I want is a simple world
with love
   and community
      and concern."

He looks at me silently,
his eyes searching my intent.
"Maybe I can help you,"
he finally answers.

"Can you?"
My voice is excited.
"I'll pay anything!"

"Oh, I have nothing for sale."

"Nothing for sale?
How can that be?"
"No, these worlds you cannot buy.
These worlds you must make."

"Make?"
No way to hide the surprise that's in my voice.

"All I have here are bits
and pieces.
You select your world.
You'll have to make it.
It's difficult
and takes a lot of time.
It would be easier
for you to go and buy
one of those ready-made worlds."

I look at the bits and pieces in confusion.
"But how do you make your own world,
especially out of all this?"
I want to give up,
but the thought of those other worlds
makes me stand fast.

"The process is long and difficult,"
he repeats.
"You will meet many discouragements.
Others will ridicule you for not simply buying
one of the other worlds.
Some people will hate you because
you make them feel uncomfortable,
or because you threaten their own worlds."
His questioning eyes ask,
"Do you want to go on?"
I nod affirmitively,
but slowly.

"It takes a great search,"
he begins.
"First you must search through these bits and pieces
for all those things you do not want.

These you must analyze carefully.
What is it made of?
   How does it work?
      Why don't you want it?
The answers are not easy.
You will often want to give up.
Sometimes the answers will frighten
and even threaten you.
If you succeed
you are ready for the next search."

He pauses, looking at me questioningly.
"Go on! Please go on!" I say.

"Now you must search
for these things which correct the bad.
This search will be extemely difficult.
Are you willing to get your hands dirty?
You will have to really dig around here,
   make many trials and errors
      throw many pieces away
         try new ones
            have successes
               have failures.
Sometimes you may wish to go back to the marketplace
and look at those other worlds again,
maybe even visit a few.
You'll want to understand them thoroughly."

Again he stops

"Go on! Please go on!"

"If you're persistent in your search,
if you really know what kind of world you want,
then your struggles will make you stronger.
You will get dirty,
   and bloody
      and so tired and discouraged;
but you will become stronger."

Now he looks at me
with a challenge in his eyes.

"Some people stop here.
They figure once they know what's right and wrong
good and bad
they've done enough.
The hardest part is just beginning.
The bits and pieces have to be put together.
You have to use those bits and pieces
to make your world!"

I squirm a bit uneasily.
"You'll get your fingers pinched,
   you'll get cut and bruised,
      sometimes it will all fall apart
         and you'll have to start over.
Others may come to destroy your world."

"Do I have to do it alone?"
I ask.
"Can't someone help me?"

He looks at me,
his eyes soothing my troubled thoughts.
"There are a few people to help;
they are back there working right now.
They are very few in number
and every now and then one of them quits.
They have been struggling for a long time
and so far their progress is very small. But . . ."
he smiles,
"They are making progress."

He takes a breath.

"It would be so much easier
to simply buy a world from
the ready-made market,
wouldn't it?"

My mind churns.
I struggle to sort out my thoughts.
I look at the piles of bits and pieces
   I look back up the alley towards the central marketplace.

"Yes,"
I say in anguish,
"It would be simpler,
but . . ."

1976

As I prepared to leave Viet Nam, I needed to somehow express my thanks to those who had accompanied me along this pilgrimage. Many of them were so involved in the task of rebuilding their country that I rarely met them any more. Others were still uncertain and afraid of what lay ahead of them. All of them were facing the challenge of how to relate to this new situation. I envied them their position. It is this kind of a challenge which helps us to grow and work through many of life's questions. I shared this poem as a farewell to my friends, and look forward to the day when we will again be together to continue the pilgrimage.

Your Dawn Is Full

Four thousand years of history are past.
You stand once more on the threshold of a new day,
as the morning sun breaks the chains of night
and casts off the burdens of darkness.
You stand before me, looking into this new dawn;
the early rays dance across the sky
casting a shiny halo about your dark hair.

Oh, to see the sunrise as you see it,
to know that it is mine,
to know that I can paint it the colors of my heart's desires,
to be able to walk hand in hand with you
into its streams of embracing light,
to share with you this glorious moment,
to know what is in your mind,
to feel what you must feel.

You have known the storms of yesterday,
but now—what strength surges through your veins
healing those bruises of days past
and urging you on to a new tomorrow.
I wish to share—
but this I know,
this sunrise is yours, and yours alone.
You hold the brush which will paint its advancing rays,
and will spread its vibrant warmth over your land.
My sunrise is elsewhere, and I must look and work for it.

And as you stand gazing at your new dawn,
and feel the strength of your new life,
I silently depart,
and leave behind a simple breath of thanks
for your smile,
your warm touch,
your shared life.
I shall always remember you standing there
with your back to me, and sun rays shimmering around you.
How I long for one last look at you
and one last tender touch;
but the dawn is too full, and the task too great
for you to dare look back now.
Look forward! Always look forward!
And someday, when I have found and painted my own sunrise,
perhaps we shall meet again under the same sky,
and walk hand in hand into the new day.

These two poems were written by a young Vietnamese girl who suddenly found herself a refugee in this foreign land.

My Heart Is Not to Be Imprisoned

This morning
as my eyes were open
for the first rays of sunlight,
homesickness again greeted me
with a sorrowful sigh.
At this far-off place
with all its
very unfamiliar faces,
I am struggling day by day
to find a warm space
to shelter myself
from all the confusions
of loving,
and frustrations of living.
Oh, God!
How am I again to face
another day
alone
and away from home?
Help me, please,
to survive these long months
and to live
these lonely days.
Please help me
to be me.
For in this strange land
I need You,
Your love, Your strength,
and Your truth
to be me.
I know my heart
is not to be imprisoned
amidst this busy material world.
It belongs to my homeland
where love can run free.   Hang

I Was in the Woods

I was in the woods
   yesterday evening.
I heard
   the water running,
   the birds singing,
   the insects murmuring.

I could even hear
   my soul weeping
   very
   very quietly.

                    Hang

Show Me the Way to Peace

Show me the way to peace
when the world is full of war.
Show me the way to forgiveness
when the world is full of liars.

Lead me to the path of love,
for life is full of hate.
Lead me to the path of hope,
for life is full of disgrace.

Teach me to have sincerity
when others learn to be greedy.
Teach me to live in harmony
when others don't want to be.

Show me when I want to follow;
lead me when I cannot see;
teach me when I don't know,
And console me when I worry.

Tieu

79